Mother of Light: The Book of Fire
Volume II
Tao of the Mother:
Cantos on Fire Eating and the Art of Love in the 21st Century

Junipur

Mother of Light Publications
2010

Copyright © 2010 Junipur
All rights reserved.

ISBN-10: 0615422195
EAN-13: 9780615422190

Dedication

This book is for Lalita Devi
and Her Persons in
Mother Meera
and
SriSri Amritanandamayi

Meera Pondicherry India 1974

SriSri Mata Amritanandamayi Devi

Acknowledgements

Special thanks and gratitude go to photographer Ellen Giamportone, for the front cover design. For more of her work please visit:
http://www.ellengiamportone.com,
and Ed Krasner, for the back cover.

Table of Contents

Prologue xi

Chapter One
The Mother 1

Chapter Two
The Wound 11

Chapter Three
The Medicine: Fire-Eating 41
    Prayer. 57
    Japa 65
    Meditation 75

Epilogue 81

ᔆ Prologue ᔆ

Dear Reader,

The writing of this book was written with express permission of Mother Meera, a universally accepted Incarnation of the Divine Mother. And it has been called "the Hour of the Mother", the 11th chime striking as I embark on the discourse; in my understanding, it is the initiation of the entirety of the human collective, on the cusp of the cosmic Age of Pisces, and that of Aquarius. The piece is meant to be a notebook about the concerns of spiritual practice in preparation for the passage, but I have entered the topic through the doorway of psychological approach – what we citizens of the 'new age' would have called "process". Among other things, I hope through the course of the journal to discuss: how psychological work, and spiritual practice are the activity of one and the same principle, differing only in name relative to the age of the aspirant, the maturity of the intent in the continuum of consciousness; that it is the agency of the Divine Mother – also named "Maha Shakti" – who comprises both the inner being pursuing the labor, as well as forming the living stream of intelligence, knowledge and power creating and guiding the birth of transformation on any point on the arc, whether it be termed "therapy", or "sadhana". And whether the goal be resolution with one's parents, integration of personality, or whole liberation of the soul from bondage.

I worried a bit when I was contemplating the writing of this book; while for me, these fields of contemplation, (and at such a pitch of intensity) are endlessly fascinating and hypnotic, I realize many find them dry, inaccessible… or worse, just pointless. If you find yourself searching for a reason to embark on some arcane study, I can but offer my own personal experience of the odyssey: I want to say spiritual practice is the pursuit of the *wild*. Beyond even instinct, it is primal, universal response to the irresistible call of the untamable, unquenchable wild. It is the human mind, in its arbitrary conceptual framework that is the finite, and the dead. But like everything in life, your interest depends on how you perceive things; how you see is, in turn, shaped and colored by what you <u>really</u> want.

It is my hope, as we are perched on a cliff overlooking the abyss, that these pages can add something fruitful to the dialogue in which we, as a people, are now engaged. But in the end, every path is a secret, inner way, singular to the unique individual. And no one knows the child but the Universal Mother – She alone possesses the book of the soul wherein is written, in letters of light, each intimate turn, step, sequence…the locks, the keys. I would not presume to outline lists of rules, or "things" to hold close. My intent has been to shed one beam on discerning the inscrutable way of the Divine Mother, as I understand it – albeit from a limited human perspective – perhaps illuminating some syllable of Her language. Best of luck to us all.

Chapter I

The Mother

"Salutations to the Supreme Goddess
Who is always auspicious.
Salutations to Her, the fundamental
Cause of this universe and
The power which sustains it.
With our full attention, we offer
Salutations to Her.

We offer our salutations to the Goddess,
Who on the one hand is terrifying
And on the other is eternally supporting
The universe.
She is the moon, and moonlight,
And the embodiment of happiness.
Salutations to Her again, and again.

She is welfare, prosperity and success.
She is both the good fortune, and
Misfortune of kings and rulers.
Salutations to Her.

> Salutations to the compassionate Goddess
> Who supports us during difficulties
> She is the essence, and the author of all
> The events of this world.
> Her complexion is dark and bluish.
>
> We offer our salutations to the Goddess,
> Who is at once the most gentle, and
> The most terrible.
> She alone is the support of the world,
> And She is the power of will.
> Salutations to Her."
>
> Fifth Mahatmya of Chandi (1)

The relationship between human psychology, as generally understood, and divine alchemy of mind and spirit, is a fascinating one. With the very recent evolution of the transpersonal arena in the study of the psyche, we have a modern effort to appreciate a spiritual dimension of man, a wholeness extending through, and beyond, the striving and aims of the personal ego. Until this time, therapeutic process had a naturally circumscribed scope of relieving the immediate presenting suffering or crisis of the personality, to enhance the comfort level, and increase functional efficacy in the world of daily activity. The arc of thought was elevated as those physicians, such as Carl Jung, came to intuit a higher calling for the "individuation" of being; with Dr. Jung's penetration into the realm of archetypal principles, "self" was perceived as a unique composition of cosmic forces, seeking harmonious balance and integration through the lens of the finite being. In this view, the spirit began to make its impress; the ego was now felt to be enveloped in the unseen, numinous realities, and influenced by them in any number of ways. So, the boundary between the terrestrial and the universal was breached once again, in the present day – but still, the perfecting of the individual self, for the benefit of its own experience, was the raison d'etre, the chief destination of the undertaking.

From the vantage point of the Divine, this might be a case of the earth asserting that it is orbited by the sun, replete with the concomitant misunderstandings implied. From Heaven down, so to speak, the ego is an ephemeral expression, gossamer as a butterfly's wing, of the omnipresent eternal Self; it has reality in a relative sense, just as the dream form has limited, though persuasive authenticity, in the context of its world. The temporal self can be seen as but a single, transient instrument in a cosmic orchestra that is forever being assembled, the host being always refined, tuned to resonate more exquisitely with the exalted chorus emanating from the primordial, infinite voice. In said perspective, the arduous undertakings we humans may perform within our troublesome beings, in service of the goals of our given lifespans, are executed for the sake of the creative manifestation of this One, and have no intrinsic existence separate from it.

The energy nexus we have termed "ego" is actually a location in the ethers; it is a vector crystallized in the grid of the subtle electrical fields that translates into waking life, as an experiment in *meaning*. The sequential incarnations to which we are committed are as ice flows in the continuum; the sum significance of these trials, like numerals in an algebraic equation, will call out for reconciliation. When, in the long trail of corporeal embodiment, the decreed volume of work is accomplished, the "I's" are dotted and the "T's" are crossed; the substance of the entire pilgrimage is rendered into tincture, the plumes of its incense wafting up to heaven. The limited one is released to leap to its final, true goal – transcendence of self. In the celestial eye, the ego *is* so that it can accrue experience; in the fulfillment and assimilation of experiencing, it outgrows its own form. What was temporary, fragmented ideation, in isolation from the whole dissolves, and becomes unified with the essence of pure meaning itself. This supreme presence has been called, throughout history, Divine Mother: She Who is Tao, All-Meaning.

> "Transformation is one aspect of the process. Transcendence, union with the Divine, is the primary aim of the human being. The goal of the Divine Personality or Avatar is to help the human being to be in the Divine. Transformation is not the final aim – but it enables all people to attain union with God more easily".
>
> Mother Meera (2)

Whether in a state of conscious awareness, or in the deep slumber of infancy, the ego body is forever in the womb of the Mother, the eternal Matrix who is our very substance, as well as the potential limitless we strain to express. Something of this nature is described in the sacred text, <u>Lalita Sahasranama</u>, <u>The Thousand Names of the Divine Mother</u>:

> "According to Sakteya (pertaining to Sakti) philosophy, the Supreme Truth and the ultimate cause of the universe are Siva-Sakti. Siva and Sakti are not distinct from each other. The Siva principle is the Essence of Consciousness devoid of attributes, without parts, actionless. Sakti is the power of action latent in that Consciousness. If Siva is Consciousness (Cit), Sakti is its embodiment. If Siva is "prakasa", the undivided Consciousness, Sakti is "vimarsa" that engenders awareness in Siva of His own existence. Sakti is inseparable from Siva as burning power from fire and light from the sun. The creation of the universe starts when Sakti emerges from Siva on its own. Sakti is all-pervading and dwells in everything. The Sakteya doctrine states that Siva, Sakti, the jiva and the Universe are intrinsically one and the same. In this doctrine, the Universe is the true manifestation of the Supreme Principle."
>
> (3)

It is to the Mother that the gestation, labor, and birth of the divine infant falls, carried out on the battlefields of human personality and soul. Let's hear the words of Sri Aurobindo, as he illuminates Her Being: (note to reader: the quotes from Aurobindo are given as he printed them; he does not always capitalize the proper pronouns for the Mother)

> ...and when the grace and protection of the Divine Mother are with you, what is there that can touch you, or whom need you fear? A little of it even will carry you through all difficulties, obstacles, and dangers; surrounded by its full presence you can go securely on your way because it is hers, careless of all menace, unaffected by any hostility however powerful, whether from this world or from worlds invisible. Its touch can turn difficulties into opportunities, failure into success, and weakness into unfaltering strength – for the grace of the Divine Mother is the Sanction of the Supreme, and now or tomorrow its effect is sure, a thing decreed, inevitable and irresistible."
>
> (4)

The Divine Mother is the living power of God forming, and <u>in</u>forming all creatures. In the life of a "worldly" man, in need of psychic or emotional aid, She may come from without, in the person of a counselor, while within, She is the intelligence that receives and actualizes counsel, to the degree to which the soul is available. In the being of a disciple, She is the inner fire of all quality necessary for deliverance: the indomitable might of will, the unquenchable flame of Love, the incandescent burning of high, discriminating vision. Every facet of Light is gathered up in Her quiver, and only the quality of the aspirant limits what can be partaken of Her boundless wealth:

> " In all that is done in the universe, the Divine through his Shakti is behind all action but he is veiled by his Yoga Maya and works through the ego of the Jiva in the lower nature. In yoga also it is the Divine who is the Sadhaka and the Sadhana; it is his Shakti with her light, power, knowledge, consciousness, Ananda, acting upon the Adhara and, when it is opened to her, pouring into it with these divine forces that makes the Sadhana possible…in proportion as the surrender and self-consecration progress the Sadhaka becomes conscious of the Divine Shakti doing the Sadhana, pouring into himself more and more of Herself, founding in him the freedom and perfection of the Divine Nature. The more this conscious process replaces his own effort, the more rapid and true his progress. But it cannot completely replace the necessity of personal effort until the surrender and consecration are pure and complete from top to bottom."

<u>The Mother</u>
Aurobindo (5)

In these hours of the tyranny of matter, we have lost the knowledge of Being. The Primordial Existing has been degraded, distorted into a miniscule reflex of "having" – this empty grasping is as close as we can usually get to approximate the experience, and access the memory of causal reality. Thus, we do not recognize the quintessential, bottomless crevasse lying between poetic metaphor and genuine, living divine quality. In our primitive conceptual framework, we may feel…"the Divine Mother <u>has</u> Joy, Love, Light…" We are no longer awake in the limitless stream of alive truth formed of direct knowledge; She does not "have" joy….the Divine Mother *Is* Joy, Peace, and every other beatitude in the universe. Yet She is not merely discrete aspects of quality, or information, but is, instead, the field of Intelligence, itself – unlimited – what was, what is, and also that which is to be. She is the hand, the brush, the paint and the canvas for the expression of the moods of God.

Ramakrishna once said that when a devotee is ready for liberation, he will be brought to the Divine Mother. One can discern how this statement sheds light on a dual function of Her nature: in the mind and soul of the aspirant, only the Mother's force can bring about the intricate final purifications, and grace-notes necessary for receptivity and release – and, from within Herself, only the Mother can give the benediction of this grace:

> "The supramental change is a thing decreed
> and inevitable in the evolution of the earth-
> consciousness; for its upward ascent is not
> ended and mind is not its last summit. But

that the change may arrive, take form and endure, there is needed the call from below with a will to recognize and not deny the Light when it comes, and there is needed the sanction of the Supreme from above. The power that mediates between the sanction and the call is the presence and power of the Divine Mother.

The Mother's power and not any human endeavor and tapasya can alone rend the lid and tear the covering and shape the vessel and bring down into this world obscurity and falsehood and death and suffering
Truth and Light and Life divine and the immortal's Ananda."

The Mother
Aurobindo (6)

Divine grace is required, first, to even evolve the sincere desire for expiation of the personal, the transient- and finally, to receive the blessing, the Holy permission to leave the stage. Or the fighting ring...or the battlefield, whatever image you prefer.

༄ Chapter II ༄

The Wound
I

    We human beings are like bleeding, oozing gashes- stigmata – in the fabric of infinity. The human not so much <u>has</u> a wound, as he <u>is</u> a wound, and the divine crisis of this tear must ultimately be met, at the point of its existential cause, to be mended. Any application or help at whatever level has its effect, everything its perfect place in the scheme, but there will come a time when the ministrations of "limited knowledge" pour salt in the grinding sorrow, and plunge the soul into a despair of helplessness. When the rings of experience have lapped, one back upon another in endless succession, and the thousands of means to cope have led to yet further entanglement or quagmire, flaying off pieces of flesh as they pass, the soul can only be satisfied with the answer lying await at the core. It is at this auspicious moment that the other sort of piercing – the precious wound of Divine grace – must be supplicated to treat the human scars of time, and karmic justice.

    But to begin with the act that opens the drama -- the crucifixion, the soul bound in time, space, and matter.... yoga has taught for millennia that climbing up the spiral staircase of the hierarchy of cause will lead you to the top rung: the phantom of duality. The eternal spirit Who submits to undergo the human spectacle enrolls, by choice, in the inestimably valuable laboratory of the 'experiment of two'. The One gains awareness of its infinite freedom and powers paradoxically, through the suffering of apparent division, loss, and the ensuing passion play of seeming-regaining. The primal wounding that is human birth, and the journey to reunion are not only meaningful, but are exalted gifts that flower into divine wisdom; to embrace this knowledge creates waves of transformation in one's basic posture in life. The compass is now set aright, the intent filled with light.

When I was young, I experienced a spontaneous kundalini awakening (see <u>Mother of Light: The Book of Fire, volume 1 The Bardo</u>), that was accompanied by many visions. In one of the earliest, I was a tiny infant, perched on the lap of a very ancient sage. He was holding open before us an immense book – it was the Book of Life – and he was pointing to the page, instructing me from it. Though this archetypal image cannot be reduced, I absorbed much, even from its outward presentation. What is most lucid is that the life we walk through is the external form of a mystic classroom and…we are each presented with the Book, like students on the first day of school. What determines the outcome of the education – be it the high marks, or mediocrity and a failing grade – will be the incoming attitude and quality of the scholar. Many now are either lacking in awareness of a curriculum, or are actively rejecting it. But the Law of the Wisdom school bends for no soul; one's elders will not be satisfied with anything less than true devotion for the coursework. Graduation from this octave to those above is awarded not to those who merely perform their tasks mechanically, or with resignation, but to those who have ripened in spirit to a state that endows them with burning love of the work. Work *is* love, and you must love the Book, to close it for the next volume...

Time is the beautiful wound of secret Love. It is all sublimely intended.

Mother Meera says, "Only the Light is real. It is difficult for the ego to accept this." As I contemplate what might be implied in Her statement, a circular reasoning is suggested; first and foremost, that the only thing that can constitute a "wound" must be a *perception* of loss of light, a diminishment of Absolute, undifferentiated radiance. So then, it is the dimming of some ultimate luminosity that gives rise to the dreaming; the imaginary worldscapes issue forth spontaneously, populated by divided selves and separate events, mindful only of their proximal reality. But it also means that all wounds are <u>dream</u> wounds; the original betrayal of reality to illusion is that light *can* be lost, or gained – or even possessed. In truth, only the Real presides.

I would like to explore some of the ways in which we, as individuals, are impacted in an immediate way by what seem to be remote philosophical abstractions. I think the most effective way to go about it is to do a little tracking of the lines of energy, as they descend from subtle to gross, much as one would follow clouds, congealing into raindrops; these, crystallizing further into the icicles we become, and move through, here in the world. Keep in mind I don't attempt a technical writing, and scripture can seem tedious and dry. Please bear with me, though, as I review briefly these general classical outlines; the diagrams must be in place, in the mind's eye, for the picture to be complete. Remember also that the words of sutras, like anything else, are external containers, only. Within them is concealed an inner light that is revealed by the Mother's touch, when the preconditions for this grace have been met. But if the vehicle, the little word-box, is what is available at a given moment, that is where we start.

The primal loss of fire that set in perpetual motion the spinning top of duality is known, in the idiom of spiritual adepts, as the 'worldly mind'. The substance, the stuff of this mind, is thought:

> "In the jiva or empirical individual, Reality or Siva or the Divine transcendental Self is Light – Bliss that is ever shining within its glory but is hidden from our gaze on account of our thought-constructs. Reality is an Eternal Presence within ourselves. It is *Siddha*, an everpresent Fact, not *sadhya*, not something to be brought into being by our efforts. It cannot be caught by our *vikalpa-jala*, by the net of our thought-constructs, however cleverly we may cast it. The more we try to catch it, the more we try to grasp it, the more does it recede from us. We are prisoners of our own mind. Thought has to commit suicide in order to know our real Self, the Siva within ourselves. *Vikalpa* 'like a dome of coloured glass stains the white Radiance of eternity'.

> When *vikalpa* ceases, the transcendental Self within us shines of itself."
>
> Siva Sutras (7)

Thought is constructed of word that, in turn, is broken down into the arrangement of letters – "matrika". It is put this way in the Siva Sutras:

> "The three kinds of *malas* or limited, vitiated knowledge are rooted in words which have a tremendous influence on our lives. These are formed of letters which are known as Matrika. The Matrika becomes the basis of all limited knowledge...<u>Matrika means unknown, unrealized mother</u>. So long as the mystery of Matrika is not realized, she is a source of bondage or limitation. When her mystery is realized, she becomes the source of liberation...These letters are not meaningless jargon. They are symbols of the creative *saktis* of the Divine. These *saktis* are collectively known as *Matrika*. This *Matrika* is the secret of all *mantras*... *Matrika* when unknown or unrealized leads to all kinds of worldly experience. When she is realized, she leads to liberation."
>
> (8)

From the fertile womb of the words, racing through the space of mind, arise the 'malas', and the condensation proceeds:

"The basis of all the three *malas* is word-bound ideas.

The words are a reflex of the letters and their sound known as *Matrika*, so ultimately it is *Matrika* which is responsible for the limited knowledge i.e., the three *malas*. Words have a tremendous influence in shaping our ideas which do not allow us to realize the Siva consciousness imprisoned within ourselves."

Siva Sutras (9)

As the word goes forth, we meet what must surely be the initial entanglement, as God dreams himself man. The Utterance is the original Cause; it is living truth. So this profound, inmost knowledge of incontrovertible might travels through the phantasm of time, into the soul of a man; now, in complete ignorance of his nature in the temporal, he innately takes as law everything he thinks, and says to himself – and others. He suffers from the faint, occluded memory of the power of the God within him, but without the freedom and perfection of that Absolute Consciousness. The intrinsic magic of the Word must undergo transformation as the Divine makes its crucial, necessary intersection with the human mentality – this, enmeshed in instinctual, animal nature in the present, and in the distortions of accumulated tendencies and karmic debris, bleeding through from the past.

To conclude the summary of these philosophical tenets, I will refer to Sri Lalita Sahasranama (The Thousand

Names of the Divine Mother) for the enunciation of the specific malas with which we grapple:

> "According to the *Saiva* scriptures, there are three types of bondages: *anupasa, bhedapasa,* and *karmapasa*. Anupasa is the misconception that the indivisible and unlimited Self is limited in some respects. This is known also as "*anava* impurity" or *anava mala (mala* is something not innate). *Bhedapasa* is seeing the Self as having many different forms. The Self is one and unique. According to *Saiva* philosophy, the root cause of seeing it as many distinct forms is *Maya*. Therefore, this bondage is also known as "*maya* impurity" or *mayamala*. *Karmapasa*, the third type of bondage, is the result of actions that cause the *jiva* to assume a body. This is also known as "*karma* impurity" or "*karmamala*."... One who frees himself of all three forms of bondage becomes Siva Himself – omniscient and omnipotent."
>
> (10)

Often in sacred writings, the process of liberation is described in images of melting – of something once artificially solid and opaque, releasing what is actually an insubstantial form, back again into the seamless ocean of consciousness. And, as is usually the case with such writings, what is interpreted as poetic, semantic metaphor to the unawakened, reveals sentient truth to the aware;

because it becomes evident, eventually, that thought is just this hardening, depicted by the sages. It is a literal freezing, from the absence of heat – the perception of personal identity, along with everything else constructed by means of thought, likewise a product of freezing, as mind falls farther, and farther from the source. If the famine of divine Fire persists, what began as a snowflake joins a glacier growing, that spreads wide and deep, into an impenetrable tundra, yawning over time without measure. To those who see beyond the cycles of manifest existence, the phenomenon is known as "samsara".

II

My wondering leads me into analysis of the pragmatic set of problems for the human race now, presenting from the scenario. In returning to the existential wound of material reality, congealing out of pure light, we naturally find that where there is injury, there is scar. If you are dealing with a fresh, immediate gash, covered with only a film of new, protective tissue, healing – reunion with essence – might be a relatively expeditious matter. Direct access is had, without additional obstruction impeding, or complicating the medicinal application. In the boyhood of man on earth, wound was simple wound, the real cause of which could be readily ascertained, and corrected. The soul of the race was nearer, in a way, to Source; the sun of the Absolute was radiating the rays of original unity into the awareness of the collective. But from here, the drama has unfolded in a trajectory that describes the procession of the "yugas" – ages of planetary consciousness – in descent into matter. Let's say Man is a warrior, passing from the morning of time into the afternoon, and evening; in his traveling, he receives into his being the arrow, tipped with the serpent venom of duality. The first split – matter from spirit, dark from light, hate from love – is buried in his chest cavity, penetrating the heart. By some weird, diabolical miracle, he doesn't drop dead straight away; he remains standing, though mortally pierced. The arrowhead beating with the heart is never detected, or removed, but instead festers. It creates deep, subterranean veins of poison that, over centuries, generate layer, upon layer of scar tissue throughout his body, even into the marrow of the bones. With every generation following him out of his loins, the toxin saturates ever more profoundly until, thousands of years later, his offspring are born with bodies, minds and hearts warped, scars already intact. Any memory or legend of the dawn, of the ancestor, and virtually any knowledge of a heart unpierced, is lost to the ages. The daily experience of these succeeding progeny, then, is the distracting, relentless battle with bodies formed by crisscrossing, hardened fibres of spiderwebs, and latticework. Who can care what started it all, in the mists of history, and what have it to do with us?

What I'm trying to get at is, under conditions such as this – such as *ours* – the wound and the scar, instead of being the natural, organic whole response of a healthy mechanism, and resolved in that simplicity, become two distinct entities; the reactive, originally protective formations are taking on lives of their own, running amok, propagating at will. Not so different than the growth of cancer cells; not other than an immune response, healing in appropriate measure, that becomes the uncontrolled killer, quite independent of the foreign invader it was called to battle. What began a life-giving temporary bandage, and <u>symptom</u> of hurt, has devolved to the status of injury in itself, obscuring completely the path back to origin.

There is a word for it – a single noun, containing within it everything that proceeds, tumbling, and gathering momentum toward oblivion, from the impaling wound of forgetting. The term, of course, is "karma". The universal flow is transparent, and empty; it has no face or form to which anything can adhere. The birth of duality is the emergence of the sticky surface of separate identity. Because this identification is accompanied by the feeling of ownership, it is compelled to experience the owning of anything that manifests out of itself, and all projection and extension of its will. Where there are 'two', there come automatically the 'ten thousand things', and the cascade wheel is in motion. Karmas arise in waves, electromagnetic storms playing across the surface of the sea; spiritual sunspots, they bind consciousness to them, and thereby to the superficial, forcefully. The more profligate the patterns in the karmic grid, the greater is the impediment to plumbing the ocean floor.

Each insult will tend to perpetuate itself, with the deepening loss of light; it will adhere to its own form, calcifying, and further diminishing the ability to utilize life experience as catalyst for potential growth. With the numbing paralysis, the true nature and depth of *original* wound is no longer felt. Rather, the raw soul power required to withstand this revelation of primal cause is buried under ash, and the necessary initiative for the essential mending – liberation – succumbs to profound slumber.

If we define "psychosis" loosely, as a psychic state existing in a perceived, but illusory isolation from 'reality', then normal human consciousness, alienated from the *fact* of undivided unity, is a psychosis at the outset – with a steeper descent into wholesale mental, spiritual illness, as the centuries have crawled over us. I can go on to make a convincing argument that the mechanism of this pandemic derangement is a dynamic of possession that likewise follows the descending spiral from subtle, to gross. When he who <u>can</u> possess is imagined out of the emptiness, the <u>possession of</u> his limitless consciousness by the projection of his fantasy – the "other"- is the inevitable result. We are utterly possessed by our minds, our emotions, obsessed by the desires and the worlds borne from them; we will eventually be owned by living entities, whether they be discarnate spirits or other people, beginning with our parents in a given life. The conglomerate of these interlopers, appearing more or less as a united front, is what we interject, and experience as our personality. We will cleave to this shady consortium more tightly than to life, in many cases; numerous sojourns in the world will be passed entirely within hermetically sealed spheres of overweening minds, now inimical to Light, that exist solely to perpetuate their far-flung creations.

Often in the modern self, the human ego is a trance that is constellated around the hub of "wound" identity. Most powerful of any configuration, the more grievous the insult, the more recalcitrant, and impenetrable the crystallization of the hypnotic dream. The entire psychology of the victim/oppressor binary, the basis of society as we recognize it, is the dramatic expression of the unshakable conviction of duality, that it proceeds to reinforce with immense fury. The rings from this signal, a stone skipped across the face of a lake, echo out as a repetition-compulsion bound to be confronted when trying to achieve purification of, and detachment from the psychic instruments. The ego self becomes hyperprotective, it grows hypervigilent against the imagined foe with a frenzied zeal, and we may eventually find ourselves encased in a closed coffin of subtle hysteria.

With wound, comes fear. Mind, the organ of control, propagates itself in direct response to terror. As threatened, or injured as we are within our beings, is as driven as we will be to manage, by diminishment, what experience comes to us; by its nature, thought works to shrink the fabric of the totality, to stem the tideswell of Absolute Reality. Earlier, I traced how this laser of mind beams out into the unknowable, like a searchlight; what it touches, it defines, <u>confines</u> by means of interpretation – but most of all, it tyrannizes. By naming, we hear the mind caught in the act of exercising its hidden endgame: this is the acquiring of Reality, itself. In asserting, we possess. Or so we hope. We must examine, catalogue, and quantify in an exhausting, ultimately futile attempt to contract, and therefore dominate. The inner being becomes progressively coarsened with falsified knowledge, and the precious quality – Amritanandamayi calls it "innocence"– is slowly destroyed. The volume of noise amplifies to a deafening din...but the light you yearn to hear is more exquisitely fine than the space between the in-breath, and the out-breath of an angel.

My mother used to refer to it as her "treasure". If you pursue far enough, you will arrive at the place where you must choose between your hurt – your righteous *right* to hurt – and the freedom, that is the absolute truth.

In my view, the ultimate goal of any work should go much beyond the near aims of balance, functionality, or comfort; the essential flower of spiritual evolution is trance-shattering. It is exorcism, in its purest form.

A compromise, or falling short of this vigil will serve to add but another layer of callous, and false security, rendering the inevitable pitched battle the more torturous. We do not want to acquiesce to a fabricated respite that will only conceal the deep seeds of betrayal within. While we execute the arduous labor of developing and refining skills of mastery in detrimental, challenging conditions, we want to hold, perhaps, the highest attribute of them all: discrimination. For just when the faculties required of the material plane are finally ours, are we most at risk of arrogance, and complacency. The pearl of great price is not of this realm; it is a power of consciousness raised to the zenith sufficient to penetrate the heavy veils of illusion, to the Supreme reality. Psychological health is a relative idea; it does not exist, at an essential level, short of realization – the return to the Light.

Mother Meera counsels that more work is done in silence. *Silence* – not the perpetual, self-creating circling around the drain of karmic theatre. This is a subtle, but deadly important point, because so easy to miss altogether, in the haze, and gunfire of your many lives: there are innumerable planes and types of work in process, at any given juncture, that may bear no outward resemblance to each other. A young aspirant may well overlook the tipping-point of the changing of the gears, when they herald a radically different application of consciousness than any with which he was, heretofore, familiar. Certainly an occupation with "material", as we call it, is a vital phase that clears and lays right, necessary foundation for future, more advanced endeavor. This analyzing, assessing and contemplating should never be avoided – which would be to forestall, to put off to gather multiplying interest, a psychic loan in the ethers. But the labor-intensive absorption with outlying temporal debts is a phase to pass through. It exists purely in service of "higher silence", that which is not attainable without the fundamental threshing of the ground of soul.

I would want to say, "do your work, master your lessons. Avoid getting <u>wedded</u> to the wound. At the end of the day, don't forget – it's all for the going home."

> "People can do nothing for my work until they themselves are realized. So all energy should go into that work of realization… What I want is complete simplicity and complete surrender, not words, not discussions, but action."
>
> Mother Meera (11)

III

I want to look a little more closely at the facts 'on the ground' of profound psychic scarring, as they pertain to the one pursuing sadhana; this is where the burden of difficulty encountered by today's seekers comes into glaring relief. An exhaustive analysis of the shapes and sizes of scars within human beings would be quite impossible – they are as numerous, varied, and distinct one from another, as the snowflakes forming that glacier. But there are, in their underlying structures, effects very much in common. As I was beginning to investigate earlier, every cut creates a barrier that inhibits receptivity; it warps, or destroys the basic capacity to receive the energies of life from the universal fountain. Damaged, in turn, is the ability to relate to the surrounding environment, a movement composed of the ebb and flow of mutual receiving and giving; the perfect circle of the eternal rhythm is shattered. This state of affairs occupies the lion's share of attention in the therapeutic setting, as well it ought, but in my experience, the devastating impact of such wounds on the delicate workings of spiritual exercise is tragically overlooked. I have found the condition of the receptive function on each level of soul to be so paramount that, should areas of impairment or destruction be neglected, or underestimated, the very fabric of the sadhana breaks down; it can be mysteriously stalled, come to a grinding halt altogether – or the road, once glowing before one's feet, can dematerialize into thin air.

It is not solely the longing, or the willingness, but the actual structural ability of the inner instrument to receive the radiation of grace, that is the all-and-everything of spiritual quest. And why? Or is it possible we have forgotten that how we <u>are</u>, relative to the Divine is...in<u> relationship</u>?

Here I suggest the reader consult the paragraphs in <u>Mother of Light: The Book of Fire, volume 1 The Bardo</u>, where a dictum arching over my particular life was revealed. First, "the superstructures of your mind are being destroyed", concluding with, "You are being made vulnerable to receive." If there is validity to what I surmise, that the scab left behind from wound has the effect of, and the express purpose to limit, to PROTECT from experience, what must this mean for the disciple? The Divine is All-Experience. What are the inevitable implications? Could we have, in our haste and hunger for the vast, leapt over the circumstance of the human heart? Now crippled, it has come to fear nothing so much as the threat of Love. Listen to the words of Meera, with these questions in mind:

> "To be open means to receive like a child – simply, with no constructions, no mind...be simple. Be like a child. The child does not know where the mother is going but loves the mother and lets her carry him, knowing that the mother will never harm him."
>
> (12)

To receive from the Mother requires a capacity for profound intimacy. To receive means to suffer yourself to be touched.

Let us pause to muse on the mystical import illuminated by Michelangelo, in the vaulted dome of the Sistine Chapel; expressed in the image of Adam and God is complete, flawless mutual reception, as the yearning finger of Adam extends to meet the outstretched finger of God. In this electric leap of true faith, on the spark that flies when the fingertips touch, creation bursts forth from the void. In the parlance of yoga, the exchange has been described, from the standpoint of our Adam, as "disciple's grace". It has been contemplated the ways in which – and the reasons, why – progress in spiritual practice will be severely limited without this dynamic; what is more, Moksha (liberation) is altogether impossible, unless the master's grace, extending out into the soul of the disciple, is met by the "grace" of the disciple, in the receiving. The circle of relationship must be completed, and the connection sealed, before the buds of divine blessing can bloom.

But an unhealed soul does not possess this faculty, nor the means to bestow it; it is comprised not only of the condition necessary to receive the benediction of God, but of the ability to deliver grace on one's own soul. For freedom. How many lifetimes will be the toll before this consummate state of wholeness has been achieved, we cannot say.

> "Many lives can go past without one taste of divine bliss."
>
> Mother Meera (13)

Now, think of yourself. Reflect, perchance, on your human mother. What was the early experience, your first association with love? Was it true? Were you safe? Is there any end to the implications of these questions? This is the age of motherless children. Robbed of the essential developmental stage of psychological and spiritual childhood by parents who frequently abdicated their own maturity, we are charged with the weight of inappropriate adulthood from birth, irrespective of our relative capacities of dispatching the responsibility. We develop with overbearing initiative, unbalanced 'self-actualization' out of harmony with the integrated whole.

Perennially discussed in the mystical forum is the immense difficulty of "controlling" the mind, restraining its frenzied, racing thoughts, to create a focal point for meditation or spiritual practice – yet one might ask, what is the mighty, roaring engine that compels the mental body, from within? It is always the lingering, clinging personal identity who speaks, without respite, in the chambers of the being across time. Today, however, we face a genuine crisis of soul: there is now a pandemic "identity sickness", passed down ancestral lineage. But not just passed, my friends; for there is tremendous variation in the quality of temporal selfhood itself, and these permutations are reflected in the collective of mankind, as the Yugas – the cosmic ages – devolve from transparent light to opaque, impermeable density. What was once "personhood", as sheer and porous to light as silk, is now an identifying code, tattooed violently into soul material. The "matrika", the letters composing the programming text, are literally scorched into being, one generation to the next, with ancient and gathering fury.

Loss of radiance is the birthplace of primal rage; lacking the leavening of illumination mind will, as a matter of course, seek to impose and reproduce its state of imprisonment on any surrounding life. Beyond forbidding the infinite nature of the child – mirroring the violence passed to the parent by <u>his</u> forbears – this rage descends into refusal of the reality of Light that is beaten into the progeny. Originally charged with educating incoming souls with the curriculum of the earth-plane challenge, those holding this power now defy divine law; they seize the throne of godhead for themselves.

And consider the insidious subtlety of the contracts, the fateful agreements forged in the preverbal unconscious matrix, flowing in blood between parent and child: the elder, incarcerated in torment, must gain the consent of the child – the reflection of his own awareness – to submit to, and protect the same imprisonment within its being, or risk violating the ' love-promise'. Such rebellion would result in summary withdrawal of the "love" and fidelity of parent to child; this, in terms of the spirit, means death.

The reader may refer here to volume 1, <u>The Bardo</u>, for an example where an extreme case is depicted: in obedience to karmic law, I absorbed into my own soul the state of demonic possession of my mother, and the concomitant obligation to resolve it. But as much as the narrative might represent high drama, the excitement of the incident in personal context is quite beside the real import of the dynamic; it writes large, in bold, shocking letters, the ring-pass-not imbedded in the consciousness of humanity, itself – relative to the individual degree of illness – as it hungers for source. In one form or another, the toxic parent commands first, "Thou shalt not be Limitless…" and then, "The Limitless shalt not exist." Should you rebel, and refuse to acquiesce, you will be renounced, to receive the sentence of certain death.

It is extremely difficult, requiring unflagging patience and perseverance to dissolve the black scar of a branding, and redeem the identity to its original pristine innocence. Such a selfhood, even if wrested away from the poisonous family matrix, will have acquired its hard-won sovereignty under severe duress. The most formidable hardship will be met as it seeks to release its personal dominance – its fiefdom – into Divine transcendence once more.

> Q: What do you feel when you see a person who has done many terrible things?....If Hitler and Saddam Hussein came to you would you give them darshan?
> MM: Yes…I see not only one person there, but many persons behind – the whole picture must be considered.
>
> Mother Meera (14)

We <u>must</u> be our own autonomy; survival depends on existing as the sole authority for ourselves, in many cases. Further, with the destruction of what is clinically termed "basic trust" in the current climate of child abuse, hypervigilence shows its face in an attachment disorder that does not permit the mentality to move forward; it is now helpless to release its guard, or its basic ownership over reality. Whatever object or ideation is in its sights will be fixated on, with life-and-death intensity, unbreakable often past the duration of the physical body. As grim and confining as this grip may be for the personality, it is absolute doom to the spiritual pursuit. Mother Meera admonishes us, "don't get stuck"; here we are, *born* stuck, in so many dimensions, while success in sadhana rests on the very capacity of the mind to separate, to depart from its familiar abode, and set forth in search of an unknown shore. Is there even a shore? We don't know, but we must dedicate and risk everything to find out.

This we cannot do, clearly, if we are locked in eternal embrace with whatever home turf – and sense of self – we have grasped for ourselves, against the adversary in our personal lives. And "individual identity" is a cloth woven from every aspect of time, place and relationship through which we have ever wandered; one cannot underestimate the truly surgical alterations to the fabric that must be experienced, in the leaving. One has to be prepared, and able, to undergo these severances.

We have never *been* children, and a day may come when we learn that we have been rendered incapable of right relation to the Divine Mother, as well. We cannot feel Her, cannot learn from Her, or interpret Her instructions. But the paramount price of this death of innocence leaves us unable to surrender to Her, right sovereign power over our souls.

The sadhana of Shakti is a form of re-mothering, from the plane of the Absolute; the Divine Mother is the universal "soul-retriever". I think we might assume, as this is food to a starving child that, it will be automatically and eagerly accepted, but I have not found it so. After a certain point, the injured seeker will not recognize, and cannot imbibe the nourishment of existence, as the long-deprived infant is helpless to eat the crust of bread. "Failure to thrive", a familiar condition in medicine, is a spiritual crisis, before it is a physical one; it makes up the barrier reef in the subtle planes that must be encountered, and resolved by those on the spiral of ascent, before the finer rungs of the ladder can be forged. I want to introduce the reality, to be elaborated on in later pages, that many of us will be led by the Divine Mother back into the profoundly karmic abyss of human hatred – its annihilations of love, and faith – so that the bridges from these little hearts to the majesty of Divine Light can be rebuilt. It is the Mother's labor to straighten or shore up the pathways, forgotten in disrepair for lifetimes, sometimes; to Her, falls the task of constructing wide, open boulevards, streaming on past mortal imagination, now radiant with Divine commerce. Finally, then, will we know what the Mother offers.

IV

Say you are a therapist of some kind; you are trying to be of help to clients who find themselves trapped in the vice of titanic clashes, plunged in a ferment of conflict and shadow. If – as some spiritual adepts have suggested – modern psychology is an infant study, of limited scope and application, what role might it play, for supplicants of the present? Well, everyone will have a different opinion on the question, expressing his, or her respective spiritual age and experience. The great metaphysical astrologer and philosopher, Dane Rudhyar, stated in one of his works, that there were two distinct avenues one could take to resolve problematic issues of mind and heart, thereby allowing the being to continue its evolution: one road was that of traditional psychotherapy, but the other, perhaps lesser known approach to psychic integration and completion was, in fact, the path of dedicated spiritual practice.

Any tool has value; but it will be put to most intelligent use if its specific qualities and parameters are fully comprehended. We observe that consciousness will find itself bound to wounds in, and of, time; these afflictions can, to some extent be addressed on the turf of time, and personal history, to begin the release of Consciousness back into eternity. There are many circumstances where a method of this type would be karmically ordained, to open the way for more profound application, later. And in addition to embarking into the preliminary chambers of the struggling awareness, a wise, well-intended therapy can certainly augment the path to the state of spiritual adulthood, so vital for higher work. We cannot know, from our human perspective, what impact is brought to bear on the goal of luminous freedom by our tiny, individual material. Can we believe the same self-loathing that condemns us to withhold succor from ourselves, in the earthly arena, will not rear its head, as the Dweller on the Threshold, when we aspire to bestow upon our hungry souls Infinity, itself? Will the transcendent glory not properly bow to the constraints of humble, transient Time, until every doorway to love has come unlocked? The heart, the will, the spirit not present in their wholeness within ourselves, are not ours to offer, in love to the divine. Any work that redeems us unto our own beings further allows the giving into union, and is a stone not to rest unturned.

As integration progresses, the solar power of love waxes; the ripening seeker will step closer to critical mass, the threshold glowing between his infinitesimal mind-world, and the unspeakable profundity. He will be torn, shredded by incomprehensible, battling forces; the irresistibility of the ascending spiral will, in the same instant, permeate his soul with the perfume of the death-longing. This intoxicating incense will distract him; it will call to him, a nightingale through the velvet dusk, until it is the only song he can hear.

The tests for the counselor, in sitting with such a client, are manifold and uncompromising; it need not be said that, generally, suicidal tendencies are symptoms of illness, or karmic injunction of a negative source – which is to say, originating in unconscious hatred. And to complicate matters, even a "mystical" longing to die motivated purely by the harkening to Light is so rare; much more common are admixtures of love and hate, swirling in a murky froth. These are pathways of 'fleeing from', the pathology treated accordingly.

But what of the ones who, in sincerity, hasten *toward*? Who are the moths, belonging to the flame? This 'divine discontent' is the apogee of the evolution to truly live, and so, of spiritual health. You might remain open to the proposition I suggest -- that the futile attempts to deny the ego's nature, with its organic endpoint, are the wrecking of psychological balance in the human population, to begin with. But can it be recognized as such, or comprehended, by the tortured patient? Will this unassuageable thirst for the death that beckons the maturing persona be discerned and honored by the physician?

What to do? Another rhetorical question, I'm afraid. If you are in the professional's chair, you will be facing the greatest challenge of your career – also, of your humanity. Just know that you confront the tenderest wish of every spirit imprisoned on earth; do your best to be knowledgeable, respectful hospice support. Perhaps you can assist your client in giving birth to enough devotion to say goodbye to this sad dream. Try to know the condition when you see it, and have compassion. No amount of brilliant technique will help; the illness is 100% fatal. In the best possible way.

(It is assumed the reader knows that physical death/suicide is not what is being referred to.)

> Q: Must the dismantling of the ego always feel like a death?

MM: To achieve realization a dying to the old self, the ego is necessary. But why be sad about it? What has the old self given you that you should love it so? The divine self will give you all things and also give you bliss. Do not think in terms of "giving up" anything. Think of "growing."

Think of always growing stronger and more loving and more complete. Then what you wanted yesterday you will not want today and what you wanted today tomorrow you will see is not useful. Discipline must be there, and control – not in the name of "death", but in the name of love and true life. You have to cut a tree sometimes to make it straight and help it grow.

Mother Meera (15)

These things said, I have noted there are those who feel the same aims can be fulfilled, and more thoroughly, by a committed spiritual practice. When considering the relative merits of these two ways it is imperative to keep our sights front and center, on the unfathomable depths of the patterns we strive to clear. According to the doctrines of yoga, every impression and tendency of nature singed into us resides encrypted in the subtle body, in the ethers, along the path of the physical spine. These 'samskaras', as they are called, hold us firmly on the mortal cross unless, and until they are incinerated by the immense heat of spiritual fire. A temporal medicine may give fleeting relief, but the offending distortion remains to surface in another shape, or form, another day – or lifetime, as it is the symptom that has been addressed, not the cause, in the soul body. Therapy proffered from one human to another, does not penetrate to the transcendent plane, where the core of the imprint – the mala – resonates. And no amount of our endeavor can mediate the Divine decree that has put the geometry of the malas in place. It is solely the power of eternity, beyond personal memory and knowledge, that will lance the poison arrow from the breast, redeeming the individual, at last, to the Limitless. The term of incarceration in time laid down on the soul by the Supreme is fulfilled, and brought to completion, by the grace of the Devi. Then the patient can rightly be pronounced "healed".

∽ Chapter III ∽

The Medicine: Fire-eating

4. Cid agni kunda sambhuta
She who was born in the fire-pit of Pure Consciousness "The nature of *Brahman* is *sat-cit-ananda*. *Cit* is the undivided *Brahman*, the ultimate source of everything. It is *jnanagni*, the fire of knowledge that burns away worldly attachments. Devi is one who came out of that fire. The undivided *Brahman* is attributeless and actionless and of that *Brahman*, Devi is the form with attributes, engaged in action…the heart (*cit*) of a *sadhak* or spiritual seeker is also a sacrificial fire-pit. Note that spiritual pursuit is called *tapas* (heat, fire). It is from the sacrificial fire that Devi arises with the radiance of a thousand suns…Fire is pictured as knowledge because it removes darkness or ignorance. It is the experience of sages that the effulgent Devi appears in the midst of the fire of knowledge to wipe out the darkness of ignorance."

Sri Lalita Sahasranama
Thousand Names of the
Divine Mother (16)

Numerous words have been spent, circumambulating the themes of loss; I have marked the trajectory, playing out in the slumber of God, from the devastating sacrifice of the Divine flame, plummeting into subterranean glaciers, now the long, icicle tusks of separate existence in which we pass our endless days. For possibly hundred of lives, and deaths, we will not possess the strength to endure the recollection of the limitless vista of our origin; the freezing will be felt as the only blessing for the inconsolable missing that is the pulse of every beat of the heart. It grows deep. The numbing must be complete; the faintest echo should be silenced. And yes, we will spend some number of lifetimes stamping out renegade sparks. We know where they come from; we know, instinctively, what it will mean if sparks, escaping control, rise into conflagration. Fire is love…and love is the death of the human ego. So it is a process of maturation – a natural function of evolution – that ordains that we cannot truly admit to, or cultivate, the Divine fire until we have exhausted the weary pleasures of our phantom selves, and are ready to die to them. Not until we recognize ourselves, in the inner sanctuaries, to be fit to undergo the inconceivable passage that was our crucifixion – in the healing, the wound is fully lived. Named the fire of "tapasya", it is the consecrated suffering the mortal man offers back to God. Tapasya is benevolent, but detached ruthlessness.

Mother Meera's guardian, Mr. Reddy, once said, "Your heart has to break to let the whole world in". A chapter on sadhana cannot begin without a closer examination of the other kind of wound than those accruing from the processes of devolution, we have been discussing. First delivered in secret – through the 'slings and arrows of the mortal coil' – and later, perfected by the exercise of sadhana, the piercing stab through the heart inflicted by the Holy is the only cure for the impaling of Time, and mortality. It is the pivotal aspect of grace we forget, or deny, in the current era. Spiritual practice is, in its essence, the divine sword, forged into its right and proper form, but more than this…for the grace stroke of the reception of the blade lies in the spiritual power to transmute the unbearable pain, the grief of the lancing, into love. It is solely through the sadhana, and the grace of the Divine thus called down, that the alchemy to transfigure the moment of death into eternal love, is bestowed.

> "Every tear is a door through which I can come. How can I come into a heart that doesn't long for me? You must love greatly to desire the great love of God. You must leave all other loves for this one."
>
> Mother Meera (17)

Meera has given the disciple the command to forget: "Forget the 'I', and you will know". There is an ancient aphorism that speaks brilliantly to the central axioms of retaining, releasing, and the complex of energies at play, in this polarity – it says: "one must dive into the ocean, not try to fill the cup". But "mind" the sphere of reality we experience, has degenerated into a condition of avarice; it is greed, vibrating on the planes of subtle energy. In today's narcissism, everything – up to, and including God – is contained by, referential to the ego, a state of affairs held to be the highest good. Profound self-giving on the spiritual level is antithetical to the culture. The instinct that informs us, whether or not we are conscious of it, is to gather and draw <u>to</u> ourselves, never to give <u>of</u> ourselves to the wider universe.

Gurumayi Chidvilasananda explained the same subtle dynamic in her analogy of the bird, sitting on a branch: she describes how the bird clings tightly to its perch, instead of letting go and flying to freedom…what a small, apparently minute gesture, like the wave of a hand. Yet the whole escape into the Limitless, of the last knot being cut, rides on this: the sigh of the breeze born as the feet release their clutch on their resting place – the branch of identity – and lift aloft, into the ethers.

'You must <u>want</u> everything' (Mother Meera): Do you *want* to forget? Could you? How many passion plays, tragedies, loves have come and gone…what number of flights out of the body into "death" will be taken, before the soul – utterly saturated, and weary – sincerely yearns only for existence, free of all identification? Not until the immense flame of eternal love comes, and fans to an uncontainable conflagration will the trivial love of the ego, for <u>itself</u>, release. It is evident, then, that the lesser light "forgets" to the extent that the greater light is "remembered".

When we reach the point of ripeness, it is the Divine Mother Who shepherds us; She is the midwife of the human soul, being reborn into eternity, as She once delivered the infant self into the crucible of time. Spiritual practice is the science of the primal relationship: of the finite heart to the infinity of spirit, of the embryonic mind to the cosmic Consciousness, of the stumbling, naked child to the limitless matrix of creation. Sadhana initiates the spiral, wending upward, through successively refined and inclusive hierarchies of intelligence. I posit from different angles in this writing that ego is fundamentally an experiment in meaning, carried out in the laboratory of soul; dedicated practice provides the exponential expansion from the specific, the focused, and the isolated, into the Totality of Meaning.

Each method of approach is its own special means to open a door from the boundless, through to the shackled moment. The Mother, always one with the separate soul in its dreamscape, must ever respect individual freedom of will; She awaits the invitation, the permission. When seeking is sincere, the contact is initiated, and tutelage begins. It is Her power – in the profound, inchoate, labyrinthine maze of the unconscious, or in flashing lightening, high across the sky of mind – that molds and chisels seeker into disciple, disciple into master. As Meera advises us,... "you must not be discouraged. You must never think, 'I cannot do this. You must know it is not you that is doing the work. It is the Mother. You must have faith in Her." (18)

Sri Aurobindo states definitively that the Divine Mother, alone, can sever the knots* ('granthis*') binding the soul life, and deliver one into the realm of Moksha. This is true simply because it is the law, and in the design of things. But, in process, it has to be understood that the trails to be traversed – the jungles, teeming with wild, charging

---
* Sanskrit term

beasts, the deserts of death, under merciless sun...or the narrow ocean channels, between sheer cliffs of gnashing razor blades – are beyond human experience to fathom, or power to negotiate. The living Cosmic Intelligence knows the way through, because She *is* the way; it is She, inherent in the body of creation, Who is the ground upon which you must tread. Without the active assistance of, and the effective partnership with the Devi, the needle will not appear before one, the eye never glimpsed. It is intrinsic to the test that the limitation of the mortal apparatus be altogether realized, appreciated, and put in proper relation to the Divine.

Sadhana is the art of love; it is the masterpiece that has no final stroke of the brush. And though the Devi, in form, can be taken as a path, as in the cases of Mother Meera and SriSri Amritananandamayi, She should not be confused with or limited to these manifestations. This would be a basic misunderstanding of the Shakti, whose fire and force becomes the topography of every journey, no matter the language, or historical basis. Read the words of the great Aurobindo, on the Divine Mother, in practice:

> "...personally too she has stooped to descend here into the Darkness that she may lead it to the Light, into the Falsehood and Error that she may convert it to the Truth, into this Death that she may turn it to godlike Life, into this world-pain and its obstinate sorrow and suffering that she may end it in the transforming ecstasy of her sublime Ananda.......but be on your guard and do

not try to understand and judge the Divine Mother by your little earthly mind that loves to subject even the things that are beyond its norms and standards, its narrow reasonings and erring impressions, its bottomless aggressive ignorance and its petty self-confident knowledge. The human mind shut in the prison of its half-lit obscurity cannot follow the many-sided freedom of the steps of the Divine Shakti. The rapidity and complexity of her vision and action outrun its stumbling comprehension; the measures of her movement are not its measures. Bewildered by the swift alteration of her many different personalities, her making of rhythms and her breaking of rhythms, her accelerations of speed and her retardations, her varied ways of dealing with the problem of one and of another, her taking up and dropping now of this line and now of that one and her gathering of them together, it will not recognize the way of the Supreme Power when it is circling and sweeping upward through the maze of the Ignorance to a supernal Light."

(19)

From the perspective of the Formless, human incarnations might be viewed as a pattern of serial polygamy; we speak sonnets of marriage vows in the attempt to bond our soul light with everything alien to its essence – to anything that is not fire. When the whiff of the absence of this intrinsic *beingness* seeps through the billowing smoke of our desires, with the searing stench of failure, we must move to the next harbinger of empty promise… to stand, in expectation, at the altar again. Zigzagging in and out of bodies, and personalities, our intermezzos are a haunted fleeing, in one direction – away from the night that lies, patiently waiting, at the heart of manifest existence. How strange it is, that the self we know is but a collection of dearly-held memories…variable expressions of time, place. But after bearing the fingerprint, and echo of uncounted, separate selves, we begin to experience a longing – obscure and unformed, in the beginning – to become the resonance of all times, all landscapes…all perfumes. All yearnings. There is no other word for "All". Behind the veils, in true stealth mode – in and around "issues" being pursued – Consciousness is being expanded, endlessly evolved, in the process of searching for Itself.

When the hour strikes for the inauguration of spiritual practice, we slowly turn, revolving in the Cosmos to face, and invoke, the Dark Night of the Soul… the nameless mystery who has been our secret companion, for these sleepless lives. Sadhana is a beckoning, a signaling of readiness for battle. An invitation onto the field, to the noble opponent. We must know, and be accountable for what is implied in our turning; there is no more 'around', or 'under' – only <u>'through'</u>.

> "Nothing must be avoided. Those who love me will work with everything in the world – all the darkness and all the difficulties. Do people imagine I do not work, or that the

realized man does not work? Divine work is the hardest work, and it is without end. I am asking people to take on the whole difficulty of matter and of Reality. I have come in a body to show that this is possible..My Grace and help and Light are there but man must also do the work. People should not come to me if they just want to escape something. I have not come only to be a refuge; I have also come to give the joy and strength necessary for change. There are no quick answers and easy solutions."

Mother Meera (20)

Practice functions to bring to bear the principle of exhaustion. The way is long. In grinding slowness, or bone-splintering suddenness, the innumerable offspring spawned by the myth of duality are drawn inexorably onto the sacrificial pyre: first, the extended family of the mind, then the mind, itself – the furtive longings of the heart, then the heart, itself. The pure cold of this material fantasy will be unmasked, and its significance thoroughly apprehended, before the dawn. It is the Divine Mother Who will bring this knowledge to you, in one hand – but in the other hand, She holds the candle, already burning, to ignite the torch of Her Presence for the voyage. The radiance of Her cosmic Sun presides in the firmament, high over the mirage of mortality, to banish the nightmares of the children of eternity.

Our walk through the worlds of spiritual practice –

those deserts, oceans, jungles and open fields – takes us to the border of and, if we are blessed, <u>through</u> a thousand veils. Sometimes we will have to make camp, holding vigil on the nearside of a particular curtain for what seems an exceeding span of time, building strength, or clarity. Every aspect of existence will ultimately be forged into a tool for the advancement of evolution, but one's innermost attitude will always determine if a fine tool is built and implemented, or whether the potential instrument lies in a heap, in the sand. Many of us will contend with lingering private agendum; we want to be cared for, for example. We intend to persist in passive, infantile and parasitic roles. We *will* to remain the "wounded one". Under the dominion of these ulterior motives, the soul will eventually be surrounded by burial mounds of wasted catalyst, multiplying into mountain ranges. What should be remembered is that each transition point comes bearing hidden crises of spiritual power, with the potential to disrupt, or possibly end the journey.

An important such curtain in the earlier stages is the flattening, distorting effect the objectifying mind will tend to have on classical concepts of spiritual works – nuts-and-bolts-ideas exactly like "mind", "ego", "detachment", "Self". Do you notice how tired, one-dimensional and *meaningless* these words become? Dusty, depressing, maybe hopeless. We have heard them to boredom, (though completely without comprehension) until the doors of perception slam shut with their very mention. As trivial a thing as it may seem – the <u>I Ching</u> would call it 'Taming Power of the Small' – there are circumstances when this sleight-of-hand conjured by… the <u>mind</u>, can capsize the ship. How daunting it is, right from the start, it's a wonder anyone penetrated to the truth; what number of souls who, feeling those germinal quickenings, were turned away by the sparse, barren appearance of the outer raiments?

If this barrier of illusion is met successfully, we will do so in ways unique to our natures. But I would enjoin a supplicant to keep several streams of thought in the forefront of the awareness, to combat the chill of falsehood: it is helpful to contemplate that we can know any spiritual terms, including those such as "sincerity", "faith" – to say nothing of "love", relative to our place on the evolutionary scale. Their *living realities* transform and articulate continually as they ascend, vibrating in the occult planes. This consciousness can aid you in piercing superficial knowledge, and associations. You can adhere to the chief assertion of the book: the MahaShakti is the keeper of the flame of meaning, within. Do not allow yourself to be dissuaded or discouraged by apparent emptiness of value or power, from the external; as the Mother teaches you to make Her glad, She will touch the letters of each word with sparks from Her fingers. They will leap up and dance, you will see. On the far side of our dry, tired thought burn the Northern Lights of the Aurora Borealis. Know it. Believe it. And press on.

A great being once said that even the amount of sadhana one is permitted is determined by karmic restriction. I want to begin this discussion with a couple of observations, to set the right tone. It is invigorating and immensely empowering to the pursuit to see it as the hard-won karmic boon it, in fact, represents, instead of as the insurmountable drudgery we might feel, at times.

Any valid practice holds keys to the sacred chambers that have been earned with blood, and tears without count. Here, at twilight, it is increasingly difficult to penetrate the descending density with conscious recognition of the mysterious powers standing in attendance, every time we sit to meditate – still, the focused, yet open concentration on what lies beyond the veils is half the battle. So it's good to undertake the work with certain knowledge of what the privilege to <u>sit</u> has cost, in the human scale of things. And to contemplate that it costs, so, because its intrinsic value, the arc of destiny it carves for the practitioner are elements known, in their entirety, to the Divine. To remember this is to open to grace. Performing sadhana always accrues the right and freedom to more sadhana – but merely the initial step, if authentic, alters forever the horizon of the soul.

At the outset of mapping the exodus from sleep to waking, Mother Meera gives sobering introductory counsel, to be hardwired into the blueprint for the approach:

> "If there is pride or vanity, then you are not awake. The really great saints and yogis are always the most humble. Humility is love; humility is what the heart knows. True joy is humble, because it is pure and given. A humble man is always quick to see his mistakes. Unless you are humble, the Divine will not use you. My power will only pass through you when you are clear – otherwise it would be dangerous for you. You must keep yourself clear at all times. The ego will

keep on trying to seize for itself what the soul is learning."

(21)

We generally critique ourselves, and one another, with intent to hurt, to diminish the being, be it overt, or disguised. Sometimes we aim to destroy. The Divine Mother, however, labors without rest to perfect the soul through the agency and power of Love, in service of the unknowable expressions of ineffable Light. We are notes in infinite stanzas, of an ever-evolving symphony; to Her falls the task of harmonizing, refining and completing the musical phrases we embody. But it is the condition of the human organism, in present day, that we furiously obstruct the reception of the divine tuning; we refuse the Holy chisel on the unformed block of marble that we are. The tangling and confusion surrounding the experience of any chastening or discipline naturally equates divine purifications with enemy assault on one's being, to be fended off at any cost.

As with all obstacles to spiritual practice, the solution is always more practice, whenever possible; the key to receiving and assimilating the sublime justice of God, when it comes, is the maturity and discrimination to discern the will – therefore, the intent – being exercised, which capacities are fruits of the work. In short, the devotion developed within your soul is the only intelligence with the power to perceive the vibrational signature of the infinite Love, wielding even the harshest sanction. Love, recognizing the mercy that is purification, receives it unto itself – thereby transmuting lead into gold.

The human persona is really a crow, attracted to a shiny object. In this era, a display of spiritual aspiration is the new status symbol among certain strata of the 'intelligentsia'. In feeding the ancient desire to ornament the personality with the transcendent beauty of spirit, loftiness of vision can be taken as plunder, to accessorize the ego; "refinement" is accumulated as coins of gold, similar to the trophy wife for a wealthy man, or a diamond ring for a woman. These appetites for ego-exaltation are especially insidious; no seeker is exempt from the virus. Alongside us, in our forays, are likely many associates within, who have no interest in the divine; they can continue on quite well without desire for truth, beyond the aggrandizement of stolen radiance. Paradoxically, though, in the sincere, the assumption is not that such distasteful defects could never be found, but that they are omnipresent and accounted for, as the occupational hazard of being human.

If you have arrived at this place, and practice is beginning, it is well to be clear on the subtle relationship between the vehicle – be it chanting, prayer, etc. – and the essence, that throne held by the Cosmic Mother, Herself.

The instrument may be the flute, but She is the breath. There are degrees of power present – no one could claim that mantram do not possess their own inherent strength – but the living Spirit will invest any practice only as that indwelling force is supplicated. And again, to the degree one is available to receive it. Like anything else in life, the highest, most classical methods will remain external, strangely empty of effect, in absence of the inner relationship between the spirit of the Mother, and the soul of the child.

∽ Prayer ∽

The uniquely tortured context of my existence provides a pointed example of proper form, but deficient in crucial connection to source. The comments in this section are distilled from personal content to illustrate the dramatic impact of a specific door, opening late in an adulthood already dedicated to other approaches: decades of meditation, kirtan (chanting), on top of many levels of shaktipat and initiation were only enough to propel my little ship into obscure deeps, and unthinkable trouble – but not to illuminate the terrain. Or deliver me to the other shore. Finally, I accrued the merit required to hear of, and then meet Meera. As was discussed in Volume 1, The Bardo, I was fascinated by Her insistence on prayer. I hadn't put thought into this way as a specific practice – I think I considered all sadhana to be forms of prayer, (which also has truth), but on reading Her injunction and commentary in the book, Answers, I built it into my work formally.

Being a complete novice in the technique, I followed Her instructions minutely: She stresses the importance of precise intent, as to the Divine being to whom the prayer is directed, (something that would never have occurred to me) as well as the clarity, and literality of that for which we ask...again, something I would not have contemplated, without being told:

"If you want anything – love, truth, or courage, for example – you must ask for it. If you ask God for anything humbly and lovingly, you will receive it. But you must ask with your whole heart, so that your heart can be empty and God can fill it. If there is pride in it, he cannot fill it as much. God wants to give you everything; you must learn how to let him.. For this you need surrender. The reward of surrender is bliss and knowledge…Ask for everything – like a child asks its mother for everything, without shame. Do not stop at peace of mind or purity of heart or surrender. Demand everything. Don't be satisfied with anything less than everything. If you ask, you will receive. If you receive, you will have to bear."

Mother Meera (22)

I don't know how peculiar this experience is to me, but when I sat for prayer, head fallen back and helpless, like a scrawny baby bird, what wasn't accomplished in thirty-years-of-everything-else slipped into the orb of my being, in a drop of golden light. The secret fire stepped forward to be met – the fire, Who was all knowledge, all facets, inflections and depths of love, every form and power of will. The flame filled the bottomless need; in the same instant, it revealed what was required to be done, so my prayers could be more exact and informed in their supplication.

With successive sessions, my consciousness was drawn in more deeply, intricately, by this pure Being – and in going, was taught how to go. I realized, along with countless, formless things, that I had never experienced the seamless, whole circle of relatedness before. Receiving and giving were waves of a single motion that was, at once, unified but dynamic, formed by one creative intelligence that bore itself new – and exponentially evolved – with every exchange. In the Catch-22 that is really perfected in sadhana, it is the Divine Mother, Herself, Who trains, equips and enables you, then, to receive Her. She renders your awareness capable of contact….the waltz goes on into the heavens, from there.

Prayer is the pure poetry of the soul, the fullness of endless articulation of the divine impulses of the Limitless. A supremely high aspect of creativity, it constellates an enormous furnace; as nothing else, prayer spins a vortex, a laser-pointed, molten state of yearning, whipped up into incendiary flame. The practice of prayer generates, distills, and then magnifies fire.

There were life-altering revelations, streams widening out into rivers – or freely floating about, as fireflies, twinkling in the night sky of summer. I was educated in configurations of wholeness, one point in the continuum sparking every other point on the sphere. An example of such a node, for me, was the introduction of the principle of "openness". To reiterate from The Bardo, Meera puts particular emphasis on the devotee praying to be open. As usual, I was full of opinions, and assumptions of how *open* I must have been, with the plethora of unusual, out-of-the-box experiences that had crowded my life, thus far.

But lucky for me, I had been brought down, and held low for so very long, eating years of desperation, I had lost much interest in my own thoughts. She is stressing this for a reason, so I just wrote the anguished plea into the litany of my prayers.

I can't adequately express what resulted, except to say it was one of the 'parting of the waters' intervals. <u>Everything</u> that came before was cleaved from everything that came after. There would, in a real sense, have been no "after" for me – no universe – had I not stated the request with conscious deliberation. The body of knowledge infused into my awareness in the months, the years that followed, revealed the great relativity of one's quality of "openness"; consider my shock and awe in discovering, in the process of <u>being</u> opened, that I had never approximated this state before, regardless of an unorthodox and strenuous span in the world. And to be taught, in no uncertain terms, that the most literate human formulation of the concept bears but a rudimentary resemblance to its rainbow-hued reality, in the body of the Divine.

The lesson came flanked by the others rushing in – the karmically complex study of what had originally engendered and comprised that fatal closing-off at the great depths, given with the significance of these individual historical factors, what ramifications and responsibilities they incurred. But more important was the initiation into the Unknown as the living, eternally present field on which sadhana is carried out. More than this, I would venture to say that It, Itself is revealed to <u>be</u> the practice. The substance, as well as the resolution of every prayer – the Unknowable – is the axis around which everything revolves like beautiful, shimmering, but weightless Christmas ornaments.

I don't want to elaborate much further on the subject of prayer to the Mother; what will be meaningful are not my words, experiences, or anyone else's, but what She will impart to you, directly within your soul, if you so choose. I might suggest that one consciously allow one's prayers to evolve; though the Devi gives according to Her wisdom always, She may signal, by an inner prompting, a particular readiness for some aspect to be heightened, an obstruction removed. I have found that with a fine-tuning of interactive communication, things can change more rapidly; the Mother will inform your prayers, if you let Her.

Before I leave off, I want to pass on a vital lesson Mother Meera puts forward in <u>Answers</u>, on the relationship between prayer, and karmic debt:

> "If we only accept our karma and act according to that, there will be no end to it – our karma will continue for many, many lives. However, if we pray and offer the fruits of our actions to the Divine, then our karma can be stopped, lessened, or transformed."
>
> (23)

This tenet instigated a really dramatic revolution in my basic attitudes, thus far. For one thing, I assumed that other limbs of sadhana in which I had previously been engaged were more directly effective on lifting the weight of karmic dross than Meera judges them to be. But, too, having started my life with somewhat dramatized knowledge of the burden I carried, my instinct was one of penance, surrender – and permanent contrition – rather than feeling it appropriate to ask for help, or relief. I would not have thought to do anything but accept the sentence with as much grace and devotion as I could muster; for those who are likewise inclined, I urge you to revise your position. It seems our responsibility is not only to suffer our fate – it is that also – but to actively seek the mercy and aid of God, and to recognize that this supplication, alone, will end the prison term.

It is well to mention the metaphysical lessons inherent in this dynamic between Time and Timeless, before closing the subject of formal entreaty to the Divine. On one hand, our loss of innocence has deprived us of knowledge of the occult power of speech that is, in many regards, received and efficacious on the subtle planes at the instant of utterance. But on the other hand, as we reside within these layered, arbitrary bands of limited reality, we must realize that karmic knots may require untying, or cutting, before we see our pleadings crystallize and bear fruit in the physical. These configurations of complexity should not go to waste for the avid student; they are not empty of significance, and do not exist sheerly to frustrate. They bear priceless secrets of the cosmic science of time and manifestation; in the threads between the prayer and its fulfillment, are waiting to be discovered mathematical equations of the relationship between dream actions, and the illusory, linear arena in which they are committed.

And so, the special boon of heartfelt prayer washes clean the doings of time and space, in the water of the boundless. We do it for our own sakes, but perhaps more for the progressive leavening that would bless the earth plane, so bowed down with toil. Think if we were lifted as a whole, in this way; we, the world, could behold the imperishable Sun of existence again.

༄ Japa ༄

"The main **shakta-upaya**, however, consists in **mantra sakti** which is inherent in Matrika and arises out of the contemplation of the Divine I-consciousness. A door gently swings open; a force arises from within which embraces our so-called 'I' to death. The limited 'I' dies to live in the universal 'I'.

Siva Sutras (24)

846. Mantra sara
She who is the essence of all mantras "'Just as all the water that falls from the sky goes to the ocean, prostration to any deity goes to Kesava'. Here we can think of the Divine Mother in place of Kesava. All deities are indeed second to the Sakti That is Mother. Thus the essence of the mantras directed toward all deities is rooted in Her."

Sri Lalita Sahasranama
The Thousand Names of
The Divine Mother (25)

Similar to prayer, the high art of mantra repetition is a method that utilizes the power of the Mother inherent in words – *matrika shakti*- in its intended place, and function. Prayer is a use of language in a profoundly intimate application, a plea reaching towards infinity, in notes and chords issuing forth from the very specific inventory of our earthly history. Not to be rigidly interpreted, but for the musing on an informative image, let's allow that the gradient of prayer is one of Time, calling out in entreaty to Eternity. Completing this equation, then, japa might be viewed as the drawing down of the flame of the eternal Absolute into the infinitesimal moment – thereby uniting with it. Put simply, the individual tongue, given to repeating the Divine Name, consumes Universal fire.

I would like to introduce these entries from the classic, Japa Yoga, by Swami Sivananda; the opening phrases are from the preface by the Divine Life Society:

> "'Yajnanam Japayajnosmi; I am the sacrifice of Japa among all sacrifices', says the Lord in the Gita. It is the continuous recitation of the Divine Name that forms the first rung in the ladder of yoga, as also the undercurrent that flows beneath the different processes of Yoga."
>
> (26)

As a dancer on a stage traces her pirouette around the unmoving "spot", so mantra japa is the "spotting point", the uniting axis around which the soul revolves in the dervish whirl of individual existence. It is the homing signal for the traveler of mind. As Mother Meera emphasizes:

> "Concerning sadhana, you must do japa when you want to receive my Light and help when I am not physically with you. Only through japa do you have constant inner contact with me. If you want to make any progress in sadhana, you must practice japa...japa is essential. Japa is not simple words – each divine name is full of divine vibrations. These surround us and protect us and penetrate both our bodies and our whole inner being. Remembrance of the divine name gives immediate peace and happiness and turns us from the worldly to the Divine. There is no special and limited time for japa. It is very good to do japa all day. If this is not possible then remember it whenever possible. We can practice japa during all activities. It is easier to remember when we do physical work without mental work. This japa helps us to purify our consciousness and makes our sadhana easy."
> (27)

Among other things, the human experience is an exercise in separation. Constructed in the pillars and mortar of personal thought, each building block is, at bottom, a recitation of our *own* name; narcissistic in nature, the act of thinking is an assertion of "i", a consolidation of the identity of our limited ego, though this 'selfness' be projected onto, and veiled in, the objects of our contemplation. In our misunderstanding of Reality, we have created rogue provinces convinced that they can, and <u>have</u>, seceded from the Union of the Divine. In its derangement, the modern mentality does not recognize anything it has not fabricated; it denies outright the reality of whatever it cannot acquire. But the mind never "acquires" the living fire of mantra...God is not possessed. The mental body can guide and direct form, but it is neither origin, nor essence. When profound impurities prevail, though, the mind is programmed to work from a basic conviction that it is creator, and sits on the throne of Divinity. Thus we have taken leave of the realm of Peace.

Mantra vibrates the whole indivisible field of reality, around and beyond the splintered multiplicity of imagination. Repetition works to balance, evolve and reconcile the apparent paradoxical poles of existence. In sadhana, through the science of japa, the 'states' are slowly drawn back together, and reincorporated into the perfect One; to repeat the Name is to give back the renegade identification from whence we thieved it. Thought is violence. Sadhana is war. Mantra brings the battle right to the adversary – the untamed mind – and the conflict heats up.

Continuing from <u>Japa Yoga</u>, there is a letter, written in long-hand, by Sri Sivanada to his devotees:

> "...Practice of japa removes the impurities of the mind, destroys sins and brings the devotee face to face with God. Japa must

become habitual. Be regular in your Japa.... Friends, the glory of the name of God cannot be established through reasoning. It can certainly be experienced through faith, devotion and constant repetition. Have reverence and faith for the name. Do not argue. Every name is filled with countless powers. Just as fire has its natural property of burning things, so also the Name of God has the power of burning the sins and desires. O Man! Take refuge in the name and cross this formidable ocean of birth and death. Name and Nami are inseparable. Glory to the Lord. Glory to His Name. Hari Om. Sri Ram."

(28)

"Do not argue." I kept the phrase anchored in my brain for years after I read it; in the interface between the practice of japa, and the human mind, this injunction is a single key that turns the tumblers of a million locks. In the studying and the walking, I have found it to be an inscrutable koan, clothed in three deceptively straightforward words. Because, in my observation, we are an argument, that has created a body through which to explore, and elaborate on its case. The fabric of our interim in the world is woven from existential statements we posit as fact: we, expressing through the shape and design of our life, say "'this' and 'that' are true". And the Absolute says, "No." Our ephemeral experience is actually a sound barrier that must be broken by the shattering vibration of the Cosmic Word.

It is the steady stream of discourse going on far beneath the surface of awareness that enforces the condition of bondage. The architecture of our core patterns that goes to comprise all-too-constricting identities resides in these levels of subtle speech that have penetrated, as radioactive particles, into planes outside the periphery of waking consciousness. There are syllables of structure – the malas – placed by the Divine, to set into motion the human drama; then there are the sounds, creating experiential reality, arising from the plays, themselves. These tones have seeped into the groundwater of soul, from lives, long gone.

Try and listen to the whispers when you go to repeat the mantra; some will be inescapably loud, disconcerting in the way that a hyperactive child will scream to drown out a mature voice. It will have quite a considerable success, too. But, continuing in the stalking of the wild gazelle of your attention, see if you can detect the wispy, barely audible, vanishing words of your questing, the interrogation of Infinity: "yes, but", or "what about this?" and "I don't _believe_". You might fall back then, in a fit of exhaustion, but just when you feel there is not strength for another thought...."but if _that's_ so, what about _this_?" Like a lawyer, hammering home a case before a judge, in the arrogant confidence that victory is assumed. And truly, with the evidentiary support of the whole material realm, weighing the scales on the side of rational analysis, one can never be too cautious. In an instant, a little red ball of "reasonable doubt" will dart off, bouncing over the hedge and down a side path, away from the silvery ropes that enclose the stage of sincere enquiry...and you're gone. How many times you return to the ring after being hoodwinked by the baying hounds of your thought, depends on your aspiration. And grace.

But deep to argument, more wistful, we are a *question* encased, for a fleeting interlude, in flesh, the very existence of which is testimony to the intrinsic asking, "What is Real?" Chances are, if you are incarnated in a body, and identified with a personality, you are still locked in heated debate with Reality, inasmuch as personality, itself, can be seen as an arbitrary appropriation – and distortion – of transcendent meaning. When we stand beneath the concentrated waterfall of japa, the mantra-shakti saturates the letters vibrating at our center; the power finally transmutes the meaning that experiences as alienated self back into Self, of pure Consciousness. It is as if in the cave of the heart of hearts gleams a wedding ring of solid gold: the script it has bourne of the random names of the legion populating this world who, by association, have defined you, melts clean in the living Fire, leaving behind the solitary engraving of your true, eternal name. Mantra is the lost world. It is the final reality that gave birth to your most poignant longing.

It is one of the innumerable beauties of japa repetition that it functions both through the positive – in affirmation – and through the negative, as well, in the form of cessation. So it is complete in asserting the limitless expanse the mind is naming, therefore merging with – the Divine Absolute – and simultaneously, in what thought is *ceasing* to create, intensify and sustain. Those profligate extensions into time, expansions into space, with the myriad tangles and webs of personality hallucinations that arise from these intersecting forces are starved of the power that vivifies. The divisions we perceive between things and beings making up the material plane, a mere mirage, are preceded by the vibration emanating from the lower, unpurified mental/emotional bodies; Omkara** dissolves this energy knot, at its center. The greater the intensity with which japa is performed, the more the essential wound of soul – splayed out on the cross of time, and space – is healed, at the point of the nailing.

And think of the metaphysical significance of "name", reflected from above, mirrored to below: "Name and Nami are one". On earth, in the body, a bride surrenders her family name; she takes her husband's as her own, to symbolize the love sacrifice of the separate self for the ideal of complete union of identity. In sadhana, the esoteric octave of the practice is revealed; in foregoing the innate promiscuity of the mind that conjugates our beings with multiple partners, we affirm, in commitment, the ultimate truth of ONE, standing alone. The bride-to-be, compelled by yearning, takes the Name of God; evoking it tirelessly, breathlessly, she attains the state of matrimony, in essence.

As your relationship to the Shakti – through mantra – evolves, your ear descends into the exceeding fine; you may even hear each "proof" being finessed, laid down unequivocally by the Mother's Light. On that distant day – when the need to question, and the boiling, underground river of energy that propels the turbulent surf is quiescent – illumination dawns. In taking the Name, you marry; and when all else is in readiness, you achieve

---

** Referring to the 'seed mantra' Om

union not only in symbol, but in truth. No longer is there a second to engender conflict, or instigate war. To your burning asking, "What is Real?", you will be receptive of the Divine answer, "I AM".

∽ Meditation ∽

I believe it was the renowned body-centered psychotherapist, Alexander Lowen, who expressed his conviction that the symptom of insomnia in a client indicated a subconscious fear of death. Death – that which extinguishes us forever, as a singular, sovereign point of reference in the universe. The great forgetting, from which we fear never again to emerge. The silent witness watching over us, as we dawdle and fritter, waiting respectfully to inscribe the final paragraph in the book of our lives. And it occurs to me that, seen from a higher curve of the spiral, what we commonly call "waking life" is none other than this: a collective, chronic condition of wild-eyed, unbroken insomnia. We are guarding anxiously against the bottomless draught of the meditative state, the stillness whose reach surpasses even the departing of consciousness from physical form.

Of the many practices, it is sitting that is met, by some, with the most entrenched, instinctive resistance; it is taken as an offensive affront to the temporal identity because, of all the ways, it is the uncompromising. In pure form, meditation offers less comforting, familiar accoutrement of word, or music to cushion. The outer sheaths of worldly context and connection are shorn; they fall away, disappearing in the depth beneath us, as we go. The place where we ultimately surrender to sit is the nexus of every path, of every sorry fantasy we have ever wandered...not knowing we are already ghosts, haunting a memory that was always empty. Our brighter dreams, as well, do not recognize they are but dimly lit, on this earth. Are we not screaming louder, and moving faster, for the express purpose of outrunning that first divine wound – the poison, spreading from the point of the arrow in the breast? When we stop, and hush, we will begin to know what we have been dying from. The root of the matter. Meditation is the beginning of death in time, and the inauguration of life in eternity. It is the conscious, intended laying down of ephemeral form, in answer to the call of Limitless Light.

The discipline of meditation, as a grand therapeutic tool, has been well-documented in recent decades. The studies have been numerous, in countries near and far; science, and psychology have confirmed what adepts have known full well through the ages, so it's not necessary to explore exhaustively what is now common knowledge; with or without reference to the Divine, or aspirations beyond the immediate palliative effect, sitting quietly, with eyes closed for a while, is good for what ails you. It can be naturally calming, mysteriously restorative. And really, many people do better with less information, or the confrontation with intimidating, ponderous concepts; their effort will bear fruit anyway, and the invisible doorway will begin to open, for future endeavors. But for those of us who start out with more profound interests, a closer look at a few aspects of meditation is rewarding.

I would like to delve a bit beneath the surface, both into the real forces at play that go to bring about these healing results, and into the crisis that the essence of the discipline presents, for some plagued with modern ills. What is spiritual practice, truly, but any means the soul may employ to present itself to the "touch"? In cooperation with the senses – or in their absence, as in meditation – the Absolute reaches through, to deliver the touch of the ineffable to the starving. We sit …and in the worlds beyond our eyes, the footsteps of our souls chart their course, back to the inestimable fullness. The mind, that 'crack in the cosmic egg' that obliterated the perfect Undivided into trillions of twisted, jagged, bloody splinters, offers its unscrupulous domain to the power of universal truth. In so doing, it is slowly brought to rest. The formless at whose gates we meditate, in fervent hopes of entering, is the womb of the Divine Mother; Her radiance, emanating from across that way, impels us from within, to travel from the outer borders – thought, personality, duality, and the 'winter of our discontent' – to essence, the Light that is perfection, joy. Forever free of waxing, or waning.

With dedication and patience, the end of sorrow, as we know it, will come – so where could there be a problem? Again, I take note of Meera's statement: as the Mother, She can give everything…but we must <u>want</u> everything. What has been studied here, at length, is precisely the unwillingness, or the inability of the human being to go to the river, and drink. I don't doubt this critical tension between human and divine was ripping us apart, even in days of greater purity and clarity. But we are in the dirge, the era of ritual sickness; the more grave the condition of the patient, the less likely will he be inclined to raise himself up, and/or the less may his constitution be able to withstand the column of light in the chamber of meditation. In the field where you sit will be drawn the centrifugal force of the Center, vibrating with the frequency belonging to the Supreme Mother. The intensity of these higher altitudes of energy can be experienced as threatening to the infirm, whose psyches lie in pieces on the ground, like an abandoned jigsaw puzzle.

Meditation is the ultimate instrument of integration. Capable of feats of harmony impossible to achieve by any outside agent, the Divine physician can perform the miraculous surgery the human doctor cannot. But, today, care should be taken with all channels of power; what was assumed in previous times – a basic level of psychological, spiritual health, providing the foundation for work with cosmic frequencies of light – is rare to find in the population of the new millennium. In our terror, we have become imprisoned on the windowpane surface of reality; we are *locked* on the outside, looking for the 'in', and have lost the capacity to negotiate the actual unknown. Meera has said that for the mind to blossom it must go beyond what it knows – but are we able? Do we possess this structural integrity and courage, anymore?

I once listened to a talk by a famous naturalist; he was speaking about a remote forest he had found, now acknowledged to be, scientifically, the quietest place on the planet. In his many treks there, he grew to observe that silence is not, as usually believed, the complete absence of sound; instead, it is the sum totality of sound, as white light is the synthesis of every color of the spectrum. In contrast, the tones that combine to make up any given ego 'sound' are few, and rigidly proscribed, as a rule; they will fight viciously to safeguard the God-given right to their inalienable distinctions.

We exist in an environment so severely warped that the mind, together with its contents, are equated with the entirety of existence; we live contaminated with a conceptual virus that deludes us that the dominion of this mentality is our only survival, to be defended whatever the cost. Victory in battle often results when the strategy "divide and conquer" is employed; likewise here, for us, what is <u>divided</u> by mind <u>is</u> conquered. To *know* things – to know *things–* has become the crutch of fearful spirits. How, then, can the natural expansion of consciousness, the quantum leap off the cliff of thought…into the breathless space of spirit be possible?

And we do not need a mere sip of water; the parched soul, dull and dusty from lifetimes of neglect, will win its luminosity again in full immersion, only. One by one, articles of clothing, garments of the self as an expression in time, drop on the shore behind us; walking to the edge, we close our eyes, and wade into the deep, disappearing. Meditation is the sacrament of baptism. The continual submersion in the water of the Absolute washes clear the stain of our ignorance. With constant practice, the effulgence of transparency is regained; the black ink spot of nescience blocks out the sun's fiery rays no longer.

What needs remembering, sometimes, is the real nature of the work – that the many things we have tried to put away from ourselves, in our carefully manicured daily awareness had not, as we had hoped, ceased to exist, in the absence of our minute conscious gaze. On the contrary, they have taken on the imponderable weight of the sinking depth, and lie in mountain ranges, in the shadows at the bottom. We close our eyes to the external, superficial brightness that the inner light of the Divine Mother may bathe our ragged souls – but we should be mindful that the flame that cleanses and gives succor, also *reveals*. In order for this magic to occur, the condemned must be named; their existence will be fully counted, welcomed back at long last, into the waiting embrace of Infinity. In the stillness, the forgotten will come loose from their watery graves, and rise to meet the magnetic radiance of Divine grace. You carry the footprints of your ancestors to the altar. We sit not just for the baptism of our prized ego selves but that the hated, the forsaken within us may receive the holy touch of redemption.

It might be redundant to say this is a difficult, occasionally dangerous enterprise. For every person who can experience healing and peace from meditation, there are probably ten who find themselves somehow repelled by its forcefield; they may be scared away by what they see, or feel. It is safe for the reasonably sound of mind,(this being a relative phrase) and it is auspicious that the practice has found general tolerance, but it is not a simple thing. (Well, actually it is, simple – but <u>we</u> are not.) In any case, for those karmically blessed with the ability to meditate, and to withstand what trial may come, true integration is possible. What other way to wholeness could there be but through the reconciliation of the universes of conscious and unconscious, split asunder across centuries? Delivered into the Mother's hands, the exalted destiny of the human being is realized, in submitting the tattered tapestry of one's existence to the celestial artistry of Her loom.

∾ Epilogue ∾

In a dream, I was poised on the tip of a diving board, floating in the vast, starlit vault of heaven. I was very sad because I had to leap off the board, to plummet into time and space, again...another incarnation. I cried, not wanting to die. But it was decreed – so I jumped, waking in the body of a child, somewhere on earth.

There can be various ways to interpret the human plight in the physical arena; your point of view might depend on where you are standing and looking out from, such as a plank in the void. More, it is determined by the direction of travel: are you coming, or going? Is it your season to build here, and harvest? Or to disassemble structures that, having fulfilled their design, will be dissolved in the ethers? The answers to these questions will tint the lens through which you observe the movie, how you clarify for yourself what it's finally about...and what part you feel born to play. In this scenario my reality was, from the beginning, an experience of the incomprehensible loss of life in eternity – a dying into time, for the sake of unfinished responsibility. The stark simplicity of the vision bears the memory, the knowledge that has permeated my 'waking' awareness, ever since – that what we endure here, for love and for duty, is not remotely *life*, but a term of entombment. Labors must be performed, a dazzling multiplicity of lessons mastered, all to prepare us for the one feat of genuine value: the exodus out of the crypt.

A central theme of the journal has been surrounding the problems of extrication; what things can aid the soul in awakening to the <u>fact</u> of its imprisonment? How best to locate and sever the ties that will so bind, once the appointed hour of return approaches? In our sabbatical here, it is Time who has presided as our master, not infinity, and it does not release us gladly. Countless journeys can be compelled, as a cost of ignorance of divine law. It was Carl Jung who said an unexamined dream is like an unopened letter, and here is my point: we are dreaming *now*. By how many cycles of return are our sentences of limitation multiplied, due to the negligence of letters left unread?

In fact, it is not for the forces of maya to free; a sword must be forged, and honed in the inferno conceived when the striving of the soul meets the grace and might of God. It is the blade, so razor sharp it can slice clean through the umbilical chord of ephemeral existence that reclaims the universal power that resides in spirit, and no other.

If we look over our sojourns from a lofty mountaintop, we will see these knotty ropes spreading out like tentacles, far and wide. Let me tell you about a friend of mine, whose tragedy concisely embodies the archetype of the mortal struggle. This dear, sad mad – let's call him "Bob"- burst into his incarnation full of confusion, disorientation, anger, trailing him in a stream of smoke, from another era. His immaturity left him with a general inability to discern his whereabouts in reality, or to decipher the educational system of the earth plane. Bob rejected the law of evolution, out of hand. His natural artistic gifts, though, blossomed early, and he found himself on the brink of great commercial success. But as luck – and karma – would have it, the mitigating factors of his psychological makeup would intrude harshly on his hopes and expectations; my friend, like Icarus, came crashing from such a height, straight into the ocean, in abysmal failure, and abject despair. His ingrained conviction that life is mean and unjust was confirmed for him; hence, he hardened into a statue of rage.

The event to which I refer took place 40 years ago. I write of it here, in the analysis of bondage, because Bob is still there. Some interval after meeting him I came to understand that, for my comrade, it was not merely a matter of daydreaming obsessively about his second 'in the sun', or dwelling on the "glory days", as they say; it was something far more serious, and threatening to him – in this life, and those to come. What I saw was a soul literally frozen in the net of time; he was abandoned, left nailed on the cross of the personal image of himself he loved the most. Bob had an idealized adoration of the world as it was then, back when he ruled the day; his starring role in that stomping ground is the only aspect of himself he can see, in his mind's eye. He is deaf to the sages, telling him that form is not spirit. That the body has no life but the transcendent, indwelling flame. He cannot see light anywhere, but in the fading ember of a dearly-held illusion. He is held motionless, in the state of mourning.

Bob is a "hungry ghost". And so are we all, in the private libraries of our hearts. The soul can be shackled in chains for any interval it chooses; in its nescience, the capacity to sleep is a power it is free to exercise, just as well as is the ability to open wide its eyes. Emanating from the immortal Soul, the heart, once anchored to the sequence of moments, exists separated from the eternal flow; it is spread across centuries, like particles of funeral ash, scattered over a thousand foreign shores. The knots tied between each jewel keep the pearls forever fixed, in isolation. The heart, beating for the passions of other days, bleeding in the pining for lost loves, is incarcerated in form; it is difficult, indeed, to achieve release, for the spirit whose innumerable faces are yet to be reunited in the single present. The I Ching refers to it as the problem of achieving the "quiet heart". You have but to observe authentic haunting, recognized in cultures around the world; in this phenomenon spirits hover and cling, sometimes hundreds of years after the body dies. These are the vapor trails of the unquiet who will eventually be drawn back into birth, a roiling wave rising up again to further their ongoing story, or pursue some resolution that had escaped them thus far. But we must be clear on a matter pivotal to the destiny of the soul: the motivating force for some well may be the finessing of a given episode, or experience – but the drive for others is the very prolonging, the continuing for its own sake, of a theme, in inability or refusal to accept definitive conclusion.

 I do believe the soul whose gaze is finally turning heavenward will find itself gathering together, by any means it can, the multicolored strands of its passages. The one primordial angel whose breath infused the pantheon of names, languages and costumes in the divine burning ground of duality will discover the power that can lift up these anguished, bereft phantoms from their burial places;

it will unite them in their true meaning, and carry them aloft, melting into light.

It is my experience that love, in Time, cannot realize the freedom for which it was first born without the holy touch from the Love, Who is infinity. Though identical in essence, the temporal can only escape its tethers by remembering its origin in the transfiguring kiss of the Divine Mother. It is the spontaneous progression of the flame, winking at the candle's tip – the mysterious, insatiable aching for every person, place and thing we have ever known – rendered indistinguishable from the fire, as it yields up its form to the incandescent resplendescence of a million suns. Who is God.

These may appear to be flowery, fantastical words, painting melodramatic images, but do not be too swift to dismiss. My concern is to leave you, in as lucid way as is possible, with an outline in the unseen realms of the metamorphosis of lesser ascending into greater, in a progression that can expand into a widening streaming... and the catalyst that can initiate, and execute the work. It is a reality that if the benediction of the Divine Mother is called down – the sadhana pursued with intensity, and unflagging commitment – time itself will bless you, setting free the doves of all the many hearts that have beat for you, in your journey here.

Mother Meera reminds us there is only one love, one energy, with no true separation anywhere. Moving forward and extrapolating from this law, it is then self-evident that we are speaking of one consciousness, any process of which is but a point in the continuum; this includes man-made studies of mind, such as psychology, and its fruits. A careful look will show plainly that the inborn intelligence, intrinsic to the whole of created life – the active agent unlocking and healing the injuries of the psyche – is the self-same force liberating that soul from the configuration of time, space and causality on a higher octave. It is none other than the Tao, the Maha Shakti. The Supreme Mother is orchestrating and operating in every surgery, each crossroad along the way, from the counsel rooms of therapy to the great caves of yoga. If you turn to Her, by any name and in whatever fashion you are able, She will receive you. Then you will know it for yourself... in the end, the only wound is sleep.

> "Realization is absolute feeling, absolute freedom to love everything and to know everything. It is the unrealized man who is like a stone; the realized man is like a bird, all life and true energy and beauty.......And when you get to the top of the mountain, then you must go down again and help others up, according to their capacities and strength. There is no rest in this work; the highest serves most lovingly; the wisest listens best; the one who has seen gives his whole life to help others to see. This is the divine way."

<u>Answers</u>
Mother Meera (29)

ŚRĪ CAKRA

Bibliography

Fifth Mahatmya of Chandi, (no text available), #1

Answers, Mother Meera, Meerama Publications, Ithaca, New York, 1991, #'s 2,11,12,13,14,15,16,17,18,20,21,22,23, 27,29

Sri Lalita Sahasranama, The Thousand Names of the Divine Mother, publ.Mata Amritananda Center, San Ramon, California, 1996, #'s 3,10,13,16,20,25

The Mother, Sri Aurobindo, publ. Sri Aurobindo Ashram, Pondicherry, India, 1994, #'s 4,5,6,19

Siva Sutras, Jaideva Singh, publ. Motilal Banarsidass, Delhi, India 1979, #'s 7,8,9, 24

www.ingramcontent.com/pod-product-compliance
Lightning Source LLC
Chambersburg PA
CBHW071725040426
42446CB00011B/2227